UNLEASH

Your Money

10 Principles To Get
Your Finances on Track

MARC COLEY

Published by:
Ellis & Ellis Consulting Group, LLC
www.ellisandellisconsulting.org
info@ellisandellisconsulting.org | 678-438-3574

ISBN 13- 978-1537234175
10- 153723417x

Printed in the United States of America.

TABLE OF CONTENTS

How to

UNLEASH

Your Money

*10 Principles To Get
Your Finances on Track*

"The most contradicting thing we can do is say we need more money but waste what we have "

- Marc Coley

PRELUDE

Listen, before we go any further, I have to make one thing crystal clear to you. The intent of this book is not to tell you what to do with your hard-earned money. However, I want to offer the many mistakes I've made pertaining to money handling - and trust me, I do mean many - as a means to prevent you from having to experience them yourself. I have offered 10 principles, or better yet 10 ideas to revamp how you think and interact with your money.

Have you ever sat and thought to yourself, "I wish I knew then, what I know now"? That was me on countless occasions, wishing I'd had more tools to make wiser decisions. With some tools in my hand, I would have made a lot of recent decisions a lot differently; I would have done everything with my future in mind. But, in hindsight, I've come to the conclusion that everything should be counted as a learning experience and a tool to push and empower others.

This book is not a guide for investing or even savings, maybe I will pen another book on that subject later — but this book is purposed to tackle the problem(s) that cause us to abuse and mishandle money in the first place. Very often, we tend to treat the "outcome" while totally omitting the root of the problem. It is similar to gardening. Whenever you only clip the weeds, instead of clipping the entire root, only a portion of the problem is treated, therefore still leaving the garden in a damage condition. How? By nature, the weed will quickly grow back, and the problem will present itself all over again. What's the remedy? It's simple: get to the root and you cure the problem.

"How To Unleash Your Money" *is* a tool that will help you uproot the weeds of faulty money handling from your financial garden. Throughout this book, I will furnish mental visuals that are easy to understand so that you are able to firmly grab the information that will change how you see, spend, and save your money.

"Where It Started for Me"

January 1st rolled in, and I was ready for 2015. You know how we get when the New Year rolls in. We start making plans of how we are going to change our life for the better. We set our resolutions and expectations in place, precisely mapping out how the year will unfold for us. We replay the last 12 months and see what we did, or better yet, what we didn't do. The first day of the year somehow brings an urgent desire to change life as it has been known. You feel as if the slate has been wiped clean and you are ready to start your new found journey.

Well, with me it was no different. I remember sitting at my computer in deep thought. At times, life demands solitude where you must sit in silence and step completely into your truth, no matter how ugly, uncomfortable, or scary it might be, and that is what I needed at that exact moment. It wasn't enjoyable, but hard thinking is healthy for us all in the long run. The more I sat, the more I started thinking about one particular area: my financial status. Here it was, I was a 26-year-old man with a stable income, but I was not financially stable in any way. Oh, the irony of it all. Sitting there thinking about what really bothered me. I continued to think, and I asked myself questions like:

What went wrong?
What happened?
What was I spending my money on?
How did I allow it to get THIS bad?
Is there any way that I can recover and get back on track?

After some more in-depth pondering, I reviewed all my debts, and I began asking myself, "How could I have been so stupid?" Let's be honest, some of the decisions we make with money are plain old stupid. If no one else wants to admit it, I will be the one to say that I've fallen prey to stupidity on more than one occasion. Even with all of the wrong money decisions that I've made, please understand that if you looked at me, you would assume that I had it all together because of how I carried myself. One look at me and you would think that I was doing great things, but in all honesty, it was all a facade. I looked better than I was doing. I remember when I was coming of age to drive, one day I passed an old crocked car lot that had a nice shiny red BMW parked and ready to sell. That day I told my dad about the car, and he laughed at the idea of me wanting it. In my mind, it seemed like a great deal, as it was reasonably priced, and it looked nice on the outside. Well, to say the least, my dad knew that the car may have looked great on the outside with shiny paint and nice tires, but the truth was that the car was more than likely a piece of junk. The sad reality of my life was that I was similar to the shiny red BMW. I looked great on the outside, but my finances were busted. I think you get the point. I was a fraud, guilty of looking the part of being wealthy, when in fact, I was broke very broke. So, at that moment, something happened that had never happened to me before. I had a light bulb experience. The light had come on, and although I was feeling very discouraged and disappointed in myself, I somehow found the strength I needed to be motivated to make some crucial changes with my finances. I have always heard people say that you won't change a situation until you get sick and tired of being sick and tired; and that was my truth. I was exhausted with being in financial bondage. It literally became overwhelming to me, so the only option for relief was to do something about it.

Marc Coley

So, I know you are more than likely thinking, *"how did you change," "what did you do?"* Well, give me a second, stop rushing me. Haha! I am going to get to the juicy part in a minute, but I have to build my foundation.

Here is the foundation:

In the year 2011, I enlisted into the military. Prior to me joining, I purchased a green 1997 Acura TL, from Atlanta, GA. It wasn't the best car by far, but it was my car, and I paid for it. Before I left, I vowed to myself that I would not get a car payment. I told myself that I would be disciplined and save my money for other things. Well, it wasn't long before I started seeing my coworkers with nice cars, and when I started making friends, I noticed that they had better cars as well, so it made me feel bad. It made me feel as if I was the odd man in the circle, like I didn't fit in well enough with the others. I had to fix that, and quickly.

You know, there is something with the wiring of humans that drives us to do whatever it takes to fix ourselves when we feel like the outcast. That is exactly what I did; I fixed myself up so I could level up with my peers. I allowed my need to fit in to push me to do something that I'd later regret. To "look the part" like everyone else, I went out, and I traded in my old Acura for a used Lincoln LS. But, here is the interesting piece to the puzzle: even though I only purchased this new car for the purpose of fitting in with the crowd, the car *wasn't* extremely expensive, and the monthly car payment *wasn't* hefty, so in actuality, I could honestly afford the car with no issue. Now, also consider this, what if everyone that I associated with had an older car? Would I have made the same decision? Would I have felt the internal pressure to upgrade? Everything is hypothetical, but I believe that I would have still had that Acura right now with no car payment.

Wow! Do you see how that pressure gets to you? Pressuring yourself to match your peers can have detrimental influence over your financial decisions if you give into it. It is pretty funny how that works. It is even funnier that no one once picked on me about my car, or said anything negative about it, yet and still, I felt "pressured" to get something new in order to be like them even though they never made me feel like being myself was an issue. I was content with my car until I found out that others had something better.

Do you see where I am going with this? If not, just sit back and wait for the other examples I have to share.

Many people don't realize this, but money handling transcends giving your card to the cashier to process a payment. It's much deeper than that. How we deal with money is interconnected with our emotions. I think many of us suffer from emotional spending--which is the act of purchasing items based on feelings rather than needs. If you take an honest evaluation of your spending history, you will probably discover that a lot of your recent purchases are more about the "reasons" you bought them than anything else. This point can be traced back to the earlier example I used about my car. The reason I purchased the car was not based on a need for something better, I purchased the car because of a feeling that I had.

While you may give yourself a good reason to justify your purchases, you always need to ask yourself this important question: why am I buying this? Am I saying that you can never buy anything just to make yourself feel good? No, of course not. I am merely saying that, when it comes to spending money, you need to know what is causing you to swipe so that you don't end up putting yourself into financial bondage. If you don't evaluate and access your spending habits, your bad habits will become extremely detrimental.

Now that you know a little about me let's dig a little deeper until we get to the root of it all.

1

Understanding Financial Roots

One of the most valuable lessons that I have learned in life is that we are truly a product of our environment. You cannot escape your foundational truths. There were certain things that shaped your intellect, your views, your opinions, and your habits. I am not saying this is bad nor good, I am simply saying that you are you, based on your environment. It doesn't matter if a chicken is a chicken, if it is raised by ducks it will respond as a duck.

Where did it all start? I mean, literally, where did it all start?

Who taught me about money?

Who showed me how to spend and/or manage money?

What was the environment I was encapsulated to like?

What indirect things did I learn about money management?

You have to ask these question to really get to the bottom of your financial woes. Why? Because every current condition is attached to a root (cause). Almost nothing just happens without something invoking it. To discover what that something is, you have to assume the responsibility to go on a search for answers. More than likely, you can probably trace your financial woes back to your childhood and upbringing. This is not to say that you can call your mom up and blast her for bad money management skills she passed along to you, whether intentionally or inadvertently. However, it is to say that you can better understand what influenced you.

When I think of roots, I think of the lifeline of something; it's a source that serves as a supplier to whatever is connected to it. Roots provide the nutrients a plant needs to survive. It also provides stability to the plant. Imagine a plant without roots. Could it grow? Could it even survive independently of its roots? There would be no way, scientifically or otherwise, that a plant could survive aside from its roots; and if there was, it would be no way that the plant would remain anchored in the soil. Given this, roots are very essential. In the same manner, I want you, for a moment, to think of your financial "roots". Understanding that roots dig deep into the earth's soil to anchor the plant, so is the same for your financial roots. There are some lessons that you learned about money, some direct and others indirect that are anchored into the soil of your mind. This way of thinking for you has damaged your ability to grow wealth, and it affects your perception of money. These ideas are hidden just as actual roots are. Your attributes are above the soil, but the foundational issues are beneath the earth. That is the area we must attack and dig up!

Many of us did not get sound information about money. For me, most lessons that I learned about money were indirect. This means that the information I learned came from things that I saw and heard, and not so much from direct teaching. My lessons were derived from external sources rather than my immediate surroundings and/or environments. The fondest memory of money is when I was about 7 or 8 years of age, and I found a $10 bill. Even though I was a child, I knew that it was of value, and I knew that the right thing to do was to return it to the rightful owner. Here's a guy that paid attention to his Barney shows!

So, I sought out to do just that, but I was informed by my aunt to not say anything but to put the money away and keep it for myself. That was a lesson, not a direct one, but an indirect one. That lesson, as a child, taught me that money is scarce and if I have it, I should always keep it for myself. As an adult that is a dangerous mindset. I know you are thinking, Why?! Doesn't that equate to just "saving your money?" No, because as a person that seeks to grow wealth, you must understand one primary wealth building secret and that is "it takes money to make money".

There is NO way that you can grow money just by merely keeping it to yourself. Rather you decide to invest in yourself or put money into the purchasing of stocks, just know that keeping it to yourself is a bad thing. Even the Bible gives the example of getting a return of what you give. Luke 6:38 instructs us to, "Give and it will be given to you".

Another money memory that I recall is hearing my grandmother speak on "not co-signing for anyone - for any reason." In addition, I remember hearing the word "credit" often, and even then, I knew that it was something that you apparently needed to keep in good standing to the best of your ability. I would often hear things about "bad credit" and this conversation would come up when someone talked about purchasing a car or financing furniture. These conversations told me that, most people have bad credit, and that for some reason it is HARD to maintain "good credit" and it also told me that co-signing was a bad thing, or could be a bad thing depending on the factors at hand.

Now all of this isn't entirely true, but as I stated earlier, the lessons were indirect, so this is simply what I interpreted from it all. Understand that everything you know at this very moment came from an external source. How mama washed her dishes is how you wash yours, how daddy wore his pants is how you wear yours, how granny cooked her cornbread is most likely how you cook yours. You get where I am going with this, EVERY lesson and perception came from something outside of yourself and when you were confronted with this information you interpreted and understood it based on your current level of knowledge at that time.

UNLEASH SESSION:

1. Dump the idea that everyone has bad credit and that's just the way it is.
2. Dump the idea that you will never be wealthy because no-one in your family is.
3. Dump the idea that you will never be out of debt.
4. Dump the idea that learning about investments is too hard to understand.
5. Dump the idea that you will die poor.
6. Dump the idea that living paycheck to paycheck is normal
7. Dump the idea that you can not save money.
8. Dump the idea that you will not thrive.
9. Dump the idea that there is a limit to your income potential.
10. Dump the idea that your finances cannot change.

Now I just took you through a crash course and trust me, I know it's not that easy to get rid of the roots that are embedded in your mind. I understand that roots are deep and being a country boy, I also understand that some roots are harder to pluck up than others. I would like for you to put this book down for a moment if you can and really go back over the dump session and replay it in your mind. Even if you have to write it down and add some more things to the list that you would like to dump. You know what roots are there better than I do. Don't worry, this is only the beginning of the process of unleashing your financial life.

The Dangers of Indirect Lessons

Let's travel for a moment back to those pesky "indirect lessons". The reason I consider them pesky is because the lesson's meaning is defined by the listener, not the teacher. When a direct lesson about money is given, you learned what the teacher wants you to know, and it is usually clear and concise. Fast forward to my adult years, I was approached by a friend of mine to consider co-signing on an apartment for him. Immediately, everything my grandmother ever said about cosigning and credit went rushing through my mind. At that moment, I heard my grandmother's voice, and I saw her face, and an unpleasant feeling overcame me. This is because all the indirect lessons I learned as a child affected me as an adult. During my childhood stages, there weren't any lessons given on money, not directly at least. We learned everything else. How to use the potty, how to be respectful, how to tie our shoe strings, and the difference between right and wrong. We learned all those things in addition to some other fundamental principles, but nothing directly on money handling. From what

I understood as a child, money came in each month from "somewhere" and we got what we wanted. I can remember begging my mom to buy me an expensive game system.

I didn't realize that money was not only for wants, but for essential needs as well. This "root" of not understanding the purpose of money is a dangerous "indirect lesson" that many adults today still struggle with. As a child, money was only used for buying things I wanted, so as an adult that same mindset affected me. I hated paying for "needs" and only wanted to use my money for wants. Could this be the reason many of us dread paying our bills but will gladly purchase a new pair of shoes and spend money on a night out on the town? Could the root be from an indirect lesson that was planted in us as a child?

This is why it is so crucial for parents to explain money and how all of it works to their children. If they fail to do so, kids would assume that money is only meant for the purpose of having fun and to appease their wants. In my eyes, when I wanted a new toy or something expensive, I didn't understand "no" because I didn't understand how things worked. From my personal experience, I believe that children should do chores to earn an allowance. I further believe that chores are a great way to instill the necessary value and discipline of money into children. Earning money is the best way to introduce a child to money management. Anything that has to be earned, is appreciated and handled carefully by the person working to earn it. I also believe that if a child has money and needs something but ask you as the parent to purchase it for them, you should use that as a time to explain that money is not only for wants but also their needs.

Parents, don't think that you should just give a child money without having something tied to it. I say that because the real world doesn't just give you money. You have to earn it, and when you have to earn something from your own hard work, you value it a lot more than when it is freely given to you. A child may not like the idea of working, but they'll also love the idea of money, and therefore, they'll work to get it as long as it's a consistent demand from you that they do so.

When I was in middle school, my aunt landed a "good-paying" job. A few times, I overheard conversations that revealed the amount of money she made from working there, and to me, I thought she was rich! Because when you're young, everything seems like a lot of money. Every weekend I would ride to a nearby city with another aunt, and I would ask for $20 bucks every week. Most times, I would go to the mall and buy a CD with the money. I can even remember thinking to myself, I am going to have a pretty big audio CD collection really soon. Other than purchasing CDs, I didn't have any real intentions for the money I'd get weekly. In all honesty, whether I purchased a CD or not, I just wanted to have $20 given to me weekly because it just felt good being able to have that amount of money on me. That was my thought process. At no time did I even have a thought remotely close to saving any of the money. I mean, not the faintest idea of putting some to the side came to me.

Consequently, the money kept coming and going just as quick; and I didn't care. I didn't care because I knew that, in a few more days, I'd get another $20. Horrible, right? What's more horrible is that this thought process carried over into my adult life, and if you are truthful to yourself, it may have carried over into your adult life as well.

As an adult, some bad habits are hard to escape and break (deep roots). Poor money handling was that bad habit for me. It was a root that was established and grew into my adulthood. I didn't value money in the least bit. I just knew that when I wanted or needed something, there would always be an outlet to get it. In retrospect, it sucks thinking about it because you can't help but think about all the money that crossed your hands as a child up until your current age, and if you were only thinking, you would be years ahead now; but the good news is, it's not too late to start! Thankfully, I've uprooted the bad roots and replaced them with new ones, and you must do the same

Marc Coley

thing!

For a second, I would like you to ponder on some things you can remember about money as a child, and how it made you feel, how it played a role in your adulthood, and what you find yourself wishing you knew then that you've come to learn now. After pondering on those things, answer the following questions.

Questions:

1. What were some direct lessons you learned about money?

2. What were some indirect lessons you learned about money?

3. What patterns have you developed as an adult that stemmed from your childhood?

4. If you have kids or plan to have children, what will you do differently than your parents did?

2
How To Determine
Convenience vs. Necessity

You are thinking it is easy to determine my needs from my wants, but I challenge you to think again. Sometimes the difference can become a bit difficult to determine because of a small but seductive thing called "conveniences". Why does a convenience store charge double for little trinkets that are priced much lower at other stores? It is because a convenient store is usually conveniently located and because of this you pay more for the "convenience" . Convenience often times attach itself to your needs and your wants. I will give you an example of when "convenience" is in effect and how it can cost you big bucks.

Let's say you are looking for your first spot. For this example, we will use an apartment instead of a home. You have finally narrowed your search between two locations. One is an apartment that is right above a shopping center and is in the center of everything. The other one is in a nice location as well, but it is not as close to the shopping areas. The one that is right above the shopping center gives you a 1 bedroom 1 bathroom for $1200.00 monthly rent while the other offers the same space for $900.00. There is a $300.00 difference between the two. Here is where things can get difficult. The convenience of the first apartment makes it more appealing to you because you are thinking that anytime you need something you could just run downstairs to get it and how cool it would be to live in such a booming location. Even though you would save money by living in the second apartment, the convenience of the first makes you question the right decision.

Convenience is the carrot that swings in front of the rabbit. It is that little temptation that blurs the decision-making process. Speaking of carrots, visit a supermarket and look at the price of a whole carrot and the price of one chopped up. There is a difference in the price because one is cut up and the other isn't.

Still not clear on how convenience works? Here is another example. Think about your cell phone. In modern days, a cell phone has become one of those things that is mandatory. So let's take a current cell phone, you have several options on how much data you are allowed each month. The more data you require, the higher your bill. In most cases, people get unlimited or very high amounts. While you don't necessarily need unlimited data, it just makes things more convenient for you when using the cell phone. You don't have to limit your usage and discipline yourself to stay under a certain amount. Therefore, you pay more money for the convenience of having more data at your disposal. That's another case of convenience costing you.

UNLEASH SESSION:

1. Understand that "regular" is not a code for something bad.

2. Find a way to be more efficient. Can you fix it yourself instead of calling someone?

3. Does it have to be new EVERY time? No, it doesn't. Used in most cases is just as good as new.

4. I think you got it now. You see the small things and perks can cost you some serious cash when you add it all up. Now if you are doing well financially and can splurge on items that you like, hey, go for it but if you are like me, you have to be mindful of the small things. Ask yourself- can I go with the "regular" and bypass the "deluxe" edition?

Questions:

1. What are some conveniences in your life? Be honest.

2. Overall, how much extra are your perks costing you each month?

3. Where could the extra money you spend on conveniences be going?

3
You Must Disconnect From Emotional Spending

Press Play - "How does it feeeeeeeel?" Yes, I sang that in my best De' Angelo voice, and so did you! Didn't you? Ha!

Spending money makes you feel good. Well, let me rephrase that. Spending money doesn't make you feel good, but purchasing items that you really like is what makes you feel good. That's a little more accurate because I don't know anyone that absolutely loves to spend money. If anything, we love buying nice and expensive things, but aren't too fond of paying for them. Right? There have been times that I go to the store and buy something just because I am bored. Wow, have you ever been in that train of thought, "where you went looking for a reason to spend money?" I know you have because that's just how we are wired.

When I traded in my car, and I rode off the lot with my new (it was used, but still new to me) Lincoln LS, I felt pretty good-- really good actually. Even though covetousness (wrongly desiring certain possessions because another person owns them) was the reason for this new car, it still felt good to me. The interior of the car was decked out with leather seats; it had a sunroof that made driving in the warm weather all the more enjoyable; and whenever the door was unlocked, it did some pretty cool things. As you can probably tell, I felt proud of my purchase, so much that I took pictures to upload to social media, and I sent a few pictures to my family members and close friends. This was a celebratory moment that I wanted to enjoy with those dearest to me.

The good spirit that came from this purchase made me give the car a name. Yeah, I named the car, but who doesn't? I named my car Cindy. Even my coworkers called her Cindy. I felt accepted. I felt good when I went places. I felt good when I pulled up to the stoplight. I enjoyed the feeling of getting out of it and looking at it, and saying to myself, "that's my car. Oh, my God! That's my car." I even enjoyed the glances that came from strangers whenever I would park the car and get out. Something about this car lifted my esteem to high levels. I felt like the man. I was so excited. Wow, who knew a car could do that? Or who knew that going to such lengths to win acceptance from others could produce such a high?

Although I had gotten the kind of high from having this car that I hadn't felt from any other source, it didn't last. The good feeling that was there in the beginning eventually faded as I started to honestly evaluate myself, my life, and my finances. I soon came to the conclusion that I had a serious financial problem on my hand. When I realized the problem I had gotten myself into, everything changed immediately.

Honest evaluation is the first step to fixing a problem. Take a moment and evaluate the purchases you've made that made you feel good, or like you were sitting on top of the world, and made others accept and embrace you a little bit more. You know, the expensive shoes, the brand name clothing, the costly outfits that win you stares as well as likes on Instagram and Facebook. Or what about the luxury car that you're driving and struggling to pay for? Or the big house in the fancy neighborhood that you honestly only moved into in order to have bragging rights? Those are all purchases that feel good initially, but become serious problems as time progresses.

Whether you realize it or not, spending money may make you feel good in a moment, but that moment will quickly dissipate. The greatest issue most people run into as it relates to money handling is not having any boundaries in place to control the money that goes out and more importantly, what it goes out for. Often, we will go to great lengths to look and feel good even when it comes at the expense of sacrificing our financial freedom and stability. This is a common and dangerous issue. Anytime you are willing to make a purchase (many times with borrowed funds from an individual or loan company) without considering how it will affect your financial stability, you are making an irresponsible decision.

Here's a key factor to keep in mind: covetousness can cost you your financial stability. Buying things to be like other people and/or to feel better about yourself isn't worth the investment, especially when you're purchasing something that you honestly can't afford. It only takes one purchase to land you in a financial ditch that can take you years to get out of. Consider that before you make another big purchase.

UNLEASH SESSION:

1. Look around your home and take mental note of why you bought some of the most expensive items. Get to the REAL reasons behind the purchase.

2. Look at your social media page and glance through some of your pictures. What were you attempting to capture in the photos? Were you only sharing a photo or did you want someone to notice how "well-off" you are?

3. Your next purchase, ask yourself why you are getting it? Is it a need? A want? Or is it because you have a point to prove to someone?

4. Stop looking for things to buy when you are bored. There are a million and one things you can do other than buying something. If you have extra money, why not place some in savings, catch up on a bill and then set a budget to "treat" yourself.

5. Don't use social media to compare your value to others.

4
No Upgrades Please

If I had three wishes from my magical financial genie, I would wish to undo my car purchases and my first official apartment purchase. Home, car, and food are one of the biggest expense that you will pay out in your life. Just imagine with me that you didn't have to pay rent/mortgage and utilities (internet, cable, power, water) or you didn't have to pay a car note, insurance each month, who would need to win the lottery? Would life be better for you? I am almost certain that it would be.

I entitled this chapter, *No Upgrades Please* because that is what I really mean. Don't upgrade the car, don't get the biggest apartment or home, and most certainly don't eat all of your money with expensive food. The biggest mistakes I made, happened when I decided to "upgrade".

I read an article recently about a guy that kept the same sneakers for a few years until he wore a hole in the sole of them, all because he wanted to save his money to go towards something else that he deemed more important. I also heard of a man keeping an old beat up Honda all because it was paid off and he didn't have a monthly expense and no matter how others felt about the car and how bad it looked, he kept it because he enjoyed not having to pay a monthly car note. He literally drove the car until it was un-drivable. What does that mean for you and me? It means that some things are way more important than the upgrade. For us the moment we are done paying for one debt, and we have free money, it's almost like our minds go into overdrive to figure out what we can purchase to take that money from us. I know this to be true because this was my mindset as well. It is as if we have become so addicted to something sucking our money that if we do not have it, we seek it out.

We are upgrade addicts. Admit it, that is the first step. No shame, I am just as guilty. It is amazing to see how mobile companies, the automobile industry, fashion industry really capitalizes on this. Let me give you a scenario that will help you better understand what I am referring to.

You and Larry are neighbors. You both have this year's latest cars. Both cars are purchased brand spanking new. You are excited for Larry, and he is excited for you. The New Year rolls in, and new car models are being advertised. No major changes, maybe some tweaks to the technology and maybe a slightly different interior. Larry gets the latest car and at that time, you can not really afford to get it. Remember your car is only about a year old now and nothing much has changed with the new model, it just looks a little different. To make matters more tempting, now you are seeing more of the latest models around town. You see it at work; you see someone at church with it. How does that make you feel?

For some, you could care less, but for most - you look at your fairly new car and all of a sudden it feels old and outdated. You feel left out of the "new car" club. You feel isolated because everyone around you has the latest and greatest and you have something that's old. Just think this all stemmed from a new option being presented. If you ever had your car serviced at a dealership, they usually try to put you into something new and that year's model. I can almost feel that is all a part of a mission to get you to come in and buy it. Nothing against the car industry, they have to make money also, but it's all on how this makes you feel.

Now, after all of the pressure, you feel you should go out and get the newer car and you know you can't really afford it, but you have to have it. You get it, and you feel great about your purchase, you can hold your head up high again because now you are back into the unofficial nonexistent new car club. This is all great, but now you have to ask yourself what will you do next year when the new model comes out? It is a vicious cycle that stops us from truly prospering, and it is not just with cars, but it exists with electronic, homes, furniture, shoes, everything!

One sure fire way to stay in financial ruins is to always upgrade. In other words, super-sizing everything in your life only because you can. We see it ALL the time in society. It's an invisible pressure and an unspoken expectation that if you have a certain amount of money your lifestyle should reflect it. If you meet someone that is a doctor, and he pulls up in a 1999 Honda accord, you question if he is really a doctor? Why? Society says that his income should be reflected in his lifestyle. The upgrade syndrome. You make more, so you spend more. If this is the case, at what moment do you give yourself a break to really build. If I am always fighting to stay above the water, at what point do I actually enjoy swimming? Life is meant to be lived without the pressures of always being in "survival mode"

UNLEASH SESSION:

1. If what you have now works, don't upgrade just because you make a few extra dollars.
2. Destroy the mindset that says your lifestyle HAS to match your income.
3. Sacrifice is the key to getting ahead; you MUST be willing to be uncomfortable for awhile for financial stability.
4. Ditch friends that "have" to be flashy, it will influence you to model their behavior.
5. "Treat yourself" when you have more than enough not

when you barely have "enough".

6. Tell 3 friends that, "you will not upgrade anything for the next _____. Ask them to make sure you stick to your word"

What Am I Facing?

It's not easy. It is just no way to put it. I know financial experts shoot out "easy steps" to turn your money around, but it's just not that simple. It's like a diet. You have to go from being able to eat what you want when you want and as often as you want to without a thought, but now you have to tell yourself no! That's a mentally daunting task.

1. Did you upgrade your car when you made more money?
2. Since your raise, do you have more breathing room financially or are things the same or worst?
3. If you got a bonus on your job, where would the money go towards?
4. Can you maintain what you have for a few years in order to reach your financial goals?
5. Do you feel pressured to live a certain type of lifestyle because of your social circle?
6. What can you NOT upgrade to save money?

5
Who Cares About Money?

Who cares about money?

Who wants to know about 401Ks? That's for old folks

Who needs to learn about IRAs and Insurance Policies?

What's there to discuss about money, other than spending or getting it?

All of the above questions reflect the dangerous mindsets that many people have concerning money. Unfortunately, this mindset can be seen especially within the younger generation. Many people don't know the significance of the above mentioned items; some know, but they don't care whatsoever. If the truth be told, knowing and not caring is just the same as not knowing at all.

The first thing we must do is get a genuine desire to learn about things that affect us most and that is our money. If you think money doesn't affect you, have a month where you don't have enough of it for food. Or better yet, your child needs money for something and you don't have the funds to cover it. In both instances you feel less of a person, you feel hopeless all because of the lack of money. So, in order to reform your mind, you must think along the lines of "why" it is important to learn because if you tell yourself that "this" is boring or that it is impossible to learn than you will be stuck right there.

Knowledge doesn't mean anything if you don't care enough to put it to use in your life. Why? Because knowledge doesn't become powerful until you make a decision to apply it. In other words, you will never see financial stability and success until you care enough to learn what you need to know about finances, and then, apply it accordingly. So many people get knowledge but never do anything with it.

Until this year, I was the one that didn't really care. I eventually learned enough about money to make wiser decisions, but I didn't care, so I didn't. That is why I am able to pen the very mind of our generation because it was my mind at one point in time. But, I grew wiser. I have never been interested in saving anything. I was interested in buying...buying...buying. Before 2015 rolled in, I was not interested in paying off any of my debts. In my mind, it was there, and it would remain there until something miraculous occurred to remove it from my credit report. As you can see, there was no sense of responsibility or urgency on my part. I simply didn't care. When you say things like "When I am rich I will pay off my debts", or "When I hit the lottery I will take care of it" shows that you are leaving your financial life up to "chance" and it also shows that you have not accepted responsibility for what you have created.

Questions I asked myself:

1. How did I manage to be employed for over 6 years without a dime saved in the bank?
2. How, at this age, am I not in a good enough space to become a home owner?
3. If I died today, what would I leave behind other than debt and sorrow?

Those questions -- well the answers to those questions -- shook me to my core. As a human being and a man, I was embarrassed. I was ashamed that I allowed myself to be so careless without any regard of how it would put a dent in my future. How could one become so caught up "living life" that they neglect to secure their own life? Not to mention, I wasn't really living at all.

Who cares about money? You should absolutely care. We should all care. If you don't care, now is a good time for you to start. If you were never taught the value of money, and that is the reason why you don't care about it, it's not too late for you to learn the ropes of finances and save yourself some unnecessary hardship.

Thinking back over the years, I can honestly say that I was never taught about money and how to be responsible with it. Most of what I know now is due to what I've learned through trial and error, and a few Google searches. Speaking of which, that reminds me of a time when I had to Google how to write a check. Isn't that horrible? Now, I've seen plenty of checks, but I didn't have a clue on how to fill one out for myself. Nowadays, checks are pretty much obsolete since we are ever evolving in this new age of technology. Still, the fact is, I was already behind in the game.

The reality is, many people have a story similar to mine. They weren't taught how to save, how to write a check, how to avoid being stuck with someone else's expenses as a result of co-signing, and so on. Beyond not being taught firsthand, many people also didn't have any examples of what it meant to be responsible when it came down to spending, saving, investing, and the like. Sadly, examples of impulsive money handling were the ones readily available.

You want to know something, though? The days of being able to use "not being taught" as an excuse are long gone. In a world where endless information is only a few clicks of a button away, being misinformed is definitely a choice. There is no reason for anyone that's at an age of understanding, and honestly cares about stewarding their finances correctly, to lack the information that is needed to be financially successful. Had I decided to take full advantage of the information that is so readily available on the internet, in books, and the like, can you imagine the number of mistakes I wouldn't have made? I most certainly can.

Speaking of mistakes. I want to share one with you: One of the biggest financial mistakes that I have made to date, was in 2011. At that time, I was in the early stages of a t-shirt company that I started called Change Culture Clothing. I started it in 2008, and it wasn't doing so well, but I maintained faith that I could pull it off. In 2011, I applied for a line of credit with my credit union. In other words, I applied for a credit card, and for some reason, I was approved. I was shocked, not really because I was approved, because I already had a credit card, but I was shocked at the amount that I was approved for. My bank, at that time, approved me for $6,500. Whaaaat? I felt rich, filthy rich! Ha!

What's a young financially ignorant entrepreneur to do with such a large amount of disposable money? Mess over it. That's exactly what I did. I wasn't worried about anything but swiping and spending. I had no clue what the interest rate was. I had no idea how I'd pay the monthly charges. All I knew was that, I had $6,500 (that belonged to someone else) to my name, and I could do whatever I wanted to with it. Having such a hefty amount of money at my fingertips came with a heap of miscalculated decisions, like the time when I convinced myself that, in order to go to the next level with my business, I needed to "look the part" and get a new website, although I already had one that worked just fine. Here I am, being careless once again. As a result of my impulsiveness, I ended up spending $5,000 on a website that I didn't like or use.

And, guess what? I'm still paying off that credit card. It's been 4 years, and the debt is still lingering.

UNLEASH SESSION:

1. Stop using the excuse of "I don't know"
2. Spend time learning about money and applying it.
3. Ensure your circle is full of people who value money and wealth building.
4. Ask questions about money, don't pretend you understand. It hurts you in the long run.

6
You Got To Keep Up

In ***"Five Ways Our Need to Fit in Controls Us",*** written by Michael W. Taft, it states that our biological wiring for group cohesion is so strong that we will do almost anything to fit in, and we are likely to feel anxiety if we don't belong. The part of this statement that grabs me is that he says that we would be willing to do almost anything to "fit in". For different people, "doing anything to fit in" looks differently, but in most instances, it absolutely includes spending money, and usually it is money that we don't have, also known as a credit card. When it came down to doing anything to fit in, or to keep up with the Jones, I wouldn't hesitate to swipe my card. My credit card was my accomplice in the crime of fitting in. If I didn't have the money, a simple swipe from my credit card always came to the rescue.

Spending makes me feel good! Let's face it, spending money gives you a good feeling, especially when it's on something that you really, really, really want. When there's an item that we have had our eyes and mind set on, we are likely to do whatever it takes to get it. Until it's in our hands, we are anxious and on the edge, and we tend to find it very difficult to go any period of time without thinking about it. As soon as we get it, however, we feel good; we feel complete and accomplished. Retail shopping is truly therapeutic and/or addictive for most people.

The phrase "retail therapy" comes to life in our consumer based society these days. We become so entangled with keeping up and satisfying our retail addiction; we don't realize what we are losing subsequently -- or we realize, but don't care enough to make responsible decisions. Feeling like we just have to have it, have to keep up, have to be the best with the latest, we allow retail to become our ruler. It's been said that the love of money is the root of all evil, and while that's certainly true, it's also true that spending money stems from that very root.

Listen, keeping up might be fun in the moment. It may win you attention, or even instant gratification on a personal level - but it will always prove to be detrimental in the long run. The issue isn't in obtaining nice things, the issue is being so committed to keeping up that your sacrifice your financial freedom in the process. Before you motion to keep up, you should ask yourself: CAN I HONESTLY AFFORD THIS PURCHASE? If your answer is no, don't make the purchase. If the answer is yes, evaluate deeper with more questions like: Can this money be better spent on something else? When's the last time I put something towards my savings account or an investment? Are all of my financial obligations met?

When you learn to stop yourself by asking important questions, you will make better decisions. A few questions will have you reconsidering what you really need to be keeping up with, rather than burying yourself in a pit because of your addiction to spending.

In addition to asking questions before making a purchase, practice being content. Don't stop at practicing, also master it. When you are content, you understand that you don't have to buy everything despite how bad you want it. Contentment teaches you that, you don't have to buy the newest model of your cell phone every time one comes out. It also teaches you that you don't have to spend extra money to purchase the newest car that you only want because it's current. In other words, **contentment gives you discipline.**

Until you become content with what you have, you will forever be stuck in the consumer wheel -- always willing to put up the big bucks to stay relevant; and guess what? -- the big companies LOVE you for it. They don't mind that you're putting yourself in the negative, because every dime you spend essentially works in their favor. This is the reason why when Black Friday and Cyber Monday rolls around, they absolutely love you and your spending habits. Why wouldn't they if they know they can count on you to spend whatever amount that will satisfy your itch to keep up and fit in?

How do you break the addiction? How do you free yourself from the notion to keep up? Well, it starts with realizing your self-worth is not tied up in material things. You are worth more than what you possess. If you never accept that revelation, you will always spend money to feel "adequate".

Everything is not what it appears to be. Trust me, I know. Just because the grass appears greener, doesn't mean that it actually is. Most times, it's just an enticing illusion designed to reel you in. I remember so vividly, the struggles of keeping up a "certain" look, when in actuality, I barely had gas money to go back and forth to work. All because I gave into the illusion that, having this "certain" look would do something significant for my life and image. Well, it didn't. In fact, the only thing I got from chasing the greener grass--that wasn't green at all--were a bunch of regrets. At one point, I was maxed out on everything. Credit cards, lines of credits, everything. I was in such a dark place.

In 2013, I decided to "treat myself". I was recovering from a strenuous deployment, and I felt somewhat entitled to something nice, so I decided to once again upgrade my car. I was almost done paying for my Lincoln LS, but I needed something that was more current and something that made a statement when I pulled up. Eventually, I decided to go ahead and get another car, even though I knew I didn't need to at the moment. To make myself feel less guilty and less irresponsible, I even justified my purchase by telling myself that I needed to upgrade before the LS started giving me problems. You know how it goes -- we will conjure up a thousand excuses to be comfortable with making a mistake.

NOTE: Have you ever noticed that when you want to make big purchases that will stretch your pockets or dent your account, you find an excuse to help you proceed with your decision? That is your common sense kicking in, in an attempt to spare you from making a bad move. Many times, we ignore that unction and follow our emotions instead.

I sold my old car and purchased an Acura TL. It was nice. I loved that car, but my love for it didn't make the situation better. That car ran me about 25 thousand dollars. My car-note went from a $100 a month to almost $500 a month, but I didn't care. I loved that car, and I looked pretty good driving it. After all, I deserved it since I had gotten a promotion at my job. A promotion meant it was only right that I got an upgraded car - right? Wrong! The truth was, I could not afford that car. The gas and the maintenance were too much for my wallet. After having it for 2 years, I tried multiple times to sell it, or to trade it in, but no one wanted to buy a 5-year-old car for the price of a new one. Trading it in wasn't an option either, because, by the time I was ready to trade it, I was upside down on the car loan. In simpler terms, I owed more on the car than it was worth. Consequently, I was stuck in a hardship all because I decided to "treat myself". That treat soon became a nightmare.

Proverbs 10:22
"The blessing of the Lord makes rich, and he adds no sorrow with it."

My treat became a nightmare quickly. It quickly went from pleasure to regret. It always amazes me that, when we buy things like cars, houses, or other expensive things, we immediately thank God for opening the door to "bless us"; but when that blessing becomes a horror story, is it still consider a blessing? Proverbs 10:22 rang loudly in my ear when I begin to clean up my finances.

God blesses us with things that we can afford, and things that will not have us scrapping to maintain it. If you're stressed out with trying to maintain a "blessing", that is a sure sign that God didn't bless you with it. You blessed yourself with it.

UNLEASH SESSION:

1. Shift your focus from just being a consumer.
2. Know you worth is not in what you have.
3. Understand that you will never have "enough" There will always be something else that you need to buy.

4. Hang around people that don't put strong emphasis on material things.

5. Be content with what you have until you reach a point where you can get better.

7
You Are Not Alone

The thing about us is that we do not like to admit the reality of things. We hate to look in the mirror of life and state what we see. Our problems with money are no different. I mean, think about it - when was the last time you have heard someone openly confess in conversation to mismanaging money? Chances are few to none. No one goes on a rant on social media saying that they have bad credit, and they are wondering how they are going to make it to payday because they are so far in the hole. Everyone pretends to have it all together, everyone pretends that their bills are paid on time, and everyone pretends that life is just peachy and fabulous when in fact there are issues present. As they always say, admitting it is the first step.

Once we admit that is an issue, then we can work to overcome it. Another thing I want you to know is that you are not alone. The biggest lie you could tell yourself about money is that you are the only one. When we feel that pressure from the idea of being the "only one" it makes things increasingly harder to overcome the challenges set before you, and I believe you can take that fact across the board to many things.

According to CNN Money, 76% of Americans are living paycheck to paycheck. Roughly three-quarters of Americans are living paycheck-to-paycheck, with little to no emergency savings, according to a survey released by Bankrate.com.

Road to Recovery

Have you ever taken a ride in your car, and after driving for a few miles down the road, you take notice of your surroundings and conclude that you're heading in the wrong direction because nothing "looks" right around you? You're not exactly sure of how to get there, but you just know that you're not going in the right direction. For all of the drivers reading this, I know you can relate. Funny enough, a life of bad spending habits feels just like that car ride. Even though you don't know the exact way you should be going, there's an internal tugging telling you that the current direction you're heading in, is not the road you should be on in order to get where you need to be.

After concluding that you're driving down the wrong road, what is the simple solution? The solution is: stop the car and find the correct road that leads to where you need to be. In the same way, this also applies to rerouting once you realize you're driving down the wrong financial road. You have to stop and locate the road to recovery. You must stop the bad habits and turn around and go the opposite direction. For you, that may mean that you'd have to stop eating out so much; stop excessive spending on things that aren't a necessity. Do you really need that new gadget? Do you really think it's a good idea to finance new tires on a car that you are still paying for?

I don't confess to being a financial guru, but what I can say is that, I have made plenty of mistakes when it comes to money, and if I don't know anything, I know what you should not do. My ultimate goal is to empower others in the area of money, and I hope that I am able to empower someone not to make the same mistakes and to also recover from the mistakes made by moving forward in a positive direction. Regardless of what it seems like, there is a road to recovery. It is very possible for you to get your finances in order, but it starts with acknowledging that you're currently on the wrong road.

Many times, our mindset is slack concerning money and wealth building. For some reason, we feel that wealth is possible for everyone except ourselves. That mindset alone is enough to deter you from the ability to be money smart. This principle is everything: "so as a man thinks so is he". Listen to me, you have the ability to come out of debt and build wealth. But, you won't be able to build wealth until you get on the road to recovery.

It all starts with you, with your mindset. Are you thinking about your future? Do you want to one day purchase a home?

Who likes living paycheck to paycheck? Who enjoys not having money to help others in need? Who enjoys not being able to contribute, financially, when there is an immediate need?

No, money isn't everything; but at the same time, it affects everything. There isn't much that you're able to accomplish without having money. In fact, one of the functions of money is to help you create a worthwhile life. If you really think about it, money determines so much. It determines if your kids will go to a good school based on the area that they live in; money determines what part of town you live in; money determines what school you go to, or what schools you can afford to send your kids to.

For the next few weeks I need you to focus on dumping all of the negative thoughts you have when it comes to getting on track financially. What you have to understand is that most of us grew up in households where "negative" thought and perception of money were unconsciously instilled in us so it is going to take some work to up root and reform our mind but it is possible. This is a critical step in getting on track with your money. Do you see how money plays a huge part in the details of our life which ultimately affects the big picture of our life? Are you ready to change? Are you ready to get on the road to recovery?

1. SET A GOAL

2. SET DEADLINES FOR THOSE GOALS

3. MINGLE WITH PEOPLE WHO CAN HOLD YOU ACCOUNTABLE.

Pay close attention to step 3. There is an old saying that goes, "if you hang around four broke people, you will be the fifth one". That's so true! It's equally true that, if you hang around four wealthy people, you just may become the fifth one. You see, the road to recovery will demand two things: a change in your surroundings and a change in your mentality. Is it is easy? No, of course not; just like it's not easy going to the gym for the summer body you've been wanting since 2 winters ago; but if you want something you have to consistently put forth an effort to obtain it. The keyword is "consistently". Consistency is a key component in getting your money in order; it's a key component to any major life change. Without it, things will remain as they are.

What does being consistent mean? That means, if you budget one month and something happens that impedes on your plan, you don't give up and say, "this isn't for me!" No, it is for you. Being broke, and in debt, isn't for you. All I am saying is, give it a try. What do you have to lose?

I will be completely honest with you. When I wrote down

everything that I owed in debt, it scared me. When I saw the number of debts, it was as if my power escaped me and I felt like there was nothing I could do to get myself above water. No matter what I felt, I didn't succumb to feeling defeated. Instead, I did the work, and step by step, I started to make progress. I changed my mindset and even though I am currently not completely out of debt, I know that it is possible, and that I am on the right track to being free.

This book is purposed to destroy the mindset of keeping up with the Jones'. It is purposed to expose you to a more well-rounded perspective, so that you'll be able to live financially free.

UNLEASH SESSION:

1. If you do not change your mind, you can not change your money.
2. Accept that you have made mistakes with money but now it is time to move forward.
3. Set Goals. Start small.

8
Your Secret Weapon

Everyone loves a secret weapon. It is that "thing" you pull out when your back is against the wall, and your opponent thinks they have the upper hand. Just as the referee is about to count you out you pull out your weapon. In this case, your secret weapon is your accountability partner. This is the most effective way to make strides in you financially recovery. In this chapter, I will lay out a few steps on how to find a financial accountability partner and how to maximize the relationship.

Can You Trust Them?

Trust is a huge thing when it comes to you and your money. Your financial status is one of those things that you don't openly let the world in on but in the case of finding a financial accountability partner you will have to find someone who you can trust with your guarded finances. You need to find a partner that you can trust to disclose your personal information to. Maybe a family member or a really good friend.

Don't Pick Your Shopping Buddy!

So you found someone you can trust, great! Now, on to the next thing. I know you are thinking, let me just ask my good friend _____ and I will gladly support you as long as it is not the same friend that you go shopping with. Your accountability partner doesn't need to be your shopping buddy or a person that tempts you to spend more money than you can afford. You know the friend I'm referring to? The friends that say, "You only live once" or the friend that says, "Stop being cheap and get the upgrade". Let's just say, you should not look in their direction when you are seeking an accountability partner. Your partner needs to be someone who is grounded financially. This means that they will keep you motivated about accomplishing your goals. They will not only encourage you, but they will also inspire you by setting and accomplishing their goals.

Are They Established Financially?

Third step in securing a good financial partner is finding someone who is on track financially. There is a saying that the blind cannot lead the blind. This is the same concept with achieving financial stability. Find someone who is ahead of you. They don't have to be a millionaire but it needs to be someone who is on track. It is good to choose someone who is ahead of you because it allows you to see someone who is doing what you are striving to achieve.

Can They Tell You The Truth?

Can they be completely honest with you? Can they tell you the truth? The person you choose needs to be an individual who has a position in your life where they can tell you the truth, and you take the truth like a champ. Doesn't need to be someone who you can easily shut out if they don't tell you what you want to hear.

These are just my suggestions on finding an accountability partner. Once you have cleared these four things, then I believe that you have successfully secured yourself a greatly accountable partner.

UNLEASH SESSION:

1. List 3 potential financial accountability partner.

    a. _____

    b. _____

    c. _____

2. Are you prepared to be completely open and honest about your financial status?

3. Can you partner tell you the complete truth without you becoming offended?

4. Allow them to check on your financial status at any time.

9
Don't Drown Helping Others

The first time on an airline, I remember listening to the safety presentation by the flight attendants, you know the one that no one listens to. I remember a very important part of the presentation, the flight attendant said that in the event of an emergency make sure that you secure your oxygen mask before you try to help your neighbor. That line has stuck with me long after that flight in 2011. To me, it said you can't help someone if you are drowning yourself. What happens is that you both are at risk of dying. The same concept applies to your financial well-being. This is a time in your life where you need to focus on rescuing yourself.

No Birthdays.

Let's face it, every week there is some type of celebration going on. There are birthdays, graduations, baby showers, and a million other things that require you to bring a "gift". In your recovery time, you have to get creative and if you are not the creative type maybe offer a free service and if that's not an option, just let your presence be enough. Sometimes we put so much pressure on ourselves to be a super friend, super uncle, and super godparents but in recovery mode, you have to learn that my presence is a present, and I am not obligated to give extra unless it is in my budget to do so. The main thing is not to put extreme pressure on yourself to get gifts.

The Family and Friends Complex

This one is difficult. It is one of the most complicated subjects when it comes to managing your money and establishing yourself financially. It is difficult because it's hard to say no to the people that you care about and somehow you feel that it is your responsibility to rescue your family/friends when they make bad financial decisions. One thing that I have learned is to say no if you can not afford to because money can easily tear a riff in relationships. Also, you have to understand that you can not be the money hero to everyone. After you lend money to everyone else and realize that now your bills are behind, who will come to your rescue? Surely it will not be the people you lent money to. So beware of not to save everyone and forget to build a nest for yourself.

Luke 6:42

How can you think of saying, 'Friend, let me help you get rid of that speck in your eye,' when you can't see past the log in your own eye? Hypocrite! First get rid of the log in your own eye; then you will see well enough to deal with the speck in your friend's eye.

UNLEASH SESSION:

1. Don't allow your family or friends to guilt you into spending money.
2. Find creative ways to help people instead of always giving money.
3. If you don't take care of your financial stability NO one else will.
4. It is perfectly ok to say "NO" and still love your friends and family.

10
Find Your Balance

Finding your balance is very critical. When I started out in the beginning of 2015, I went in headstrong. I was doing everything in my power to clear out debts. I stopped eating out, refused to go shopping, and was trying to sell my car. Anything in my power to catch up financially I was willing and ready. Now this is by no means a bad thing because I was doing something good, but even in doing something good, you can go about it the wrong way. I will give you this example.

Imagine if you wanted to improve your health and you started going to the gym faithfully every day. Now this is good, and you are motivated, but this approach can be dangerous. Even in working out you have to give your body its proper time to heal and recover from the stress that you are putting on it. So in the case of your money, you have to find balance, that means that you have to set a budget that includes a "cheat day" or, "cheat allowance". There needs to be money in your budget to just do whatever you want to do with it. It doesn't need to be money that you use to pay a bill. The logic behind this is that if you are following your goals and you are knocking out things, there has to be space for a reward or in the terms of a gym head, there needs to be a "cheat day".

UNLEASH SESSION:

1. Cheat days are allowed.

2. Budget your "cheat money".

3. Set your own pace for saving money.

4. Keep track of your victories so that you stay motivated.

So what are you waiting for, **Go Unleash Your Money!**

Contact Information

If you would like more information on how to contact Certified Financial Counselor, Marc Coley please visit:

Website: www.mymoneyunleashed.com

E-mail: info@mymoneyunleashed.com.

building your business, one block at a time

Book Publishing
Graphic Design
Ministry Branding
Business Consultants

www.ellisandellisconsulting.org
info@ellisandellisconsulting.org
(954)-439-0760

64438030R00037

Made in the USA
Charleston, SC
27 November 2016